DECADENCE

DECADENCE

HENRY SIDGWICK MEMORIAL
LECTURE

by

The Right Hon.
ARTHUR JAMES BALFOUR, M.P.

[DELIVERED AT NEWNHAM COLLEGE,
JANUARY 25, 1908]

CAMBRIDGE
at the University Press
1908

CAMBRIDGE
UNIVERSITY PRESS

University Printing House, Cambridge CB2 8BS, United Kingdom

Published in the United States of America by Cambridge University Press, New York

Cambridge University Press is part of the University of Cambridge.

It furthers the University's mission by disseminating knowledge in the pursuit of education, learning and research at the highest international levels of excellence.

www.cambridge.org
Information on this title: www.cambridge.org/9781107425712

First published 1908
First paperback edition 2014

A catalogue record for this publication is available from the British Library

ISBN 978-1-107-42571-2 Paperback

DECADENCE.

I MUST begin what I have to say with a warning and an apology. I must warn you that the present essay makes no pretence to be an adequate treatment of some compact and limited theme; but rather resembles those wandering trains of thought, where we allow ourselves the luxury of putting wide-ranging questions, to which our ignorance forbids any confident reply. I apologise for adopting a course which thus departs in some measure from familiar precedent. I admit its perils. But it is just possible that when a subject, or group of subjects, is of great inherent interest, even a tentative, and interrogative, treatment of it may be worth attempting.

My subject, or at least my point of departure, is Decadence. I do not mean the sort of decadence often attributed to certain phases of artistic or literary development, in which an overwrought technique, straining to express sentiments too subtle or too morbid, is deemed to have supplanted the direct inspiration of an earlier and a simpler age. Whether these autumnal glories, these splendours touched with death, are recurring phenomena in the literary cycle: whether, if they be, they are connected with other forms of decadence, may be questions well worth asking and answering. But they are not the questions with which I am at present concerned. The decadence respecting which I wish to put questions is not literary or artistic, it is political and national. It is the decadence which attacks, or is alleged to attack, great communities and historic civilisations: which is to societies of men what senility is to man, and is often, like senility, the precursor and the cause of final dissolution.

It is curious how deeply imbedded in ordinary discourse are traces of the conviction that childhood, maturity, and old age, are stages in the corporate, as they are in the individual, life. "A young and vigorous nation," "a decrepit and moribund civilisation"—phrases like these, and scores of others containing the same implication, come as trippingly from the tongue as if they suggested no difficulty and called for no explanation. To Macaulay (unless I am pressing his famous metaphor too far) it seemed natural that ages hence a young country like New Zealand should be flourishing, but not less natural that an old country like England should have decayed. Berkeley, in a well-known stanza, tells how the drama of civilisation has slowly travelled westward to find its loftiest development, but also its final catastrophe, in the New World. While every man who is weary, hopeless, or disillusioned talks as if he had caught these various diseases from the decadent epoch in which he was born.

But why *should* civilisations thus wear out and great communities decay? and what evidence is there that in fact they do? These questions, though I cannot give to them any conclusive answers, are of much more than a merely theoretic interest. For if current modes of speech take decadence more or less for granted, with still greater confidence do they speak of Progress as assured. Yet if both are real they can hardly be studied apart, they must evidently limit and qualify each other in actual experience, and they cannot be isolated in speculation.

Though antiquity, Pagan and Christian,

took a different view, it seems easier, *a priori*, to understand Progress than Decadence. Even if the former be limited, as presumably it is, by the limitation of human faculty, we should expect the ultimate boundary to be capable of indefinite approach, and we should *not* expect that any part of the road towards it, once traversed, would have to be retraced. Even in the organic world, decay and death, familiar though they be, are phenomena that call for scientific explanation. And Weismann has definitely asked how it comes about that the higher organisms grow old and die, seeing that old age and death are not inseparable characteristics of living protoplasm, and that the simplest organisms suffer no natural decay, perishing, when they do perish, by accident, starvation, or specific disease.

The answer he gives to his own question is that the death of the individual is so useful to the race, that Natural Selection has, in all but the very lowest species, exterminated the potentially immortal.

One is tempted to enquire, whether this ingenious explanation could be so modified as to apply not merely to individuals but to communities. Is it needful for the cause of civilisation as a whole, that the organised embodiment of each particular civilisation, if and when its free development is arrested, should make room for younger and more vigorous competitors? And if so can we find in Natural Selection the mechanism by which the principle of decay and dissolution shall be so implanted in the very nature of human associations that a due succession among them shall always be maintained?

To this second question the answer must, I think, be in the negative. The struggle for existence between different races and different societies has admittedly played a great part in social development. But to extend Weismann's idea from the organic to the social world, would imply a prolonged competition between groups of communities in which decadence was the rule, and groups in which it was not ;—ending in the survival of the first, and the destruction of the second. The groups whose members suffered periodical decadence and dissolution would be the fittest to survive : just as, on Weismann's theory, those species gain in competitive efficiency whom death has unburdened of the old.

Few will say that in the petty fragment of human history which alone is open to our inspection, there is satisfactory evidence of any such long drawn process. Some may even be disposed to ask whether there is adequate evidence of such a phenomenon as decadence at all. And it must be acknowledged that the affirmative answer should be given with caution.

Evidently we must not consider a diminution of national power, whether relative or absolute, as constituting by itself a proof of national decadence. Holland is not decadent because her place in the hierarchy of European Powers is less exalted than it was two hundred and fifty years ago. Spain was not necessarily decadent at the end of the seventeenth century because she had exhausted herself in a contest far beyond her resources either in money or in men. It would, I think, be rash even to say that Venice was decadent at the end of the eighteenth century, though the growth of other Powers, and the diversion of the great trade routes, had shorn her of wealth and international influence. These are misfortunes which in the sphere of sociology correspond to accident or disease in the sphere of biology. And what we are concerned to know is whether in the sphere of sociology there is also anything corresponding to the decay of old age—a decay which may be hastened by accident or disease, which must be ended by accident or disease, but is certainly to be distinguished from both.

However this question should be answered the cases I have cited are sufficient to shew where the chief difficulty of the enquiry lies. Decadence, even if it be a reality, never acts in isolation. It is always complicated with, and often acts through, other more obvious causes. It is always therefore possible to argue that to these causes, and not to the more subtle and elusive influences collectively described as 'decadence,' the decline and fall of great communities is really due.

Yet there are historic tragedies which (as it seems to me) do most obstinately refuse to be thus simply explained. It is in vain that historians enumerate the public calamities which preceded, and no doubt contributed to, the final catastrophe. Civil dissensions, military disasters, pestilences, famines, tyrants, tax-gatherers, growing burdens, and waning wealth —the gloomy catalogue is unrolled before our eyes, yet somehow it does not in all cases wholly satisfy us: we feel that some of these diseases are of a kind which a vigorous body politic should easily be able to survive, that others are secondary symptoms of some obscurer malady, and that in neither case do they supply us with the full explanations of which we are in search.

Consider for instance the long agony and final destruction of Roman Imperialism in the West, the most momentous catastrophe of which we have historic record. It has deeply stirred the imagination of mankind, it has been the theme of great historians, it has been much explained by political philosophers, yet who feels that either historians or philosophers have laid bare the inner workings of the drama? Rome fell, and great was the fall of it.   But why it fell, by what secret mines its defences were breached, and what made its garrison so faint-hearted and ineffectual—this is not so clear.

In order to measure adequately the difficulty of the problem let us abstract our minds from historical details and compare the position of the Empire about the middle of the second century, with its position in the middle of the third, or again at the end of the fourth, and ask of what forces history gives us an account, sufficient in these periods to effect so mighty a transformation.   Or, still better, imagine an observer equipped with our current stock of political wisdom, transported to Rome in the reign of Antoninus Pius or Marcus Aurelius, and in ignorance of the event, writing letters to the newspapers on the future destinies of the Empire. What would his forecast be ?

We might suppose him to examine, in the

first place, the military position of the State, its probable enemies, its capacities for defence. He would note that only on its eastern boundary was there an organised military Power capable of meeting Rome on anything like equal terms, and this only in the regions adjacent to their common frontier. For the rest he would discover no civilised enemy along the southern boundary to the Atlantic or along its northern boundary from the Black Sea to the German Ocean. Warlike tribes indeed he would find in plenty : difficult to crush within the limits of their native forests and morasses, formidable it may be in a raid, but without political cohesion, military unity, or the means of military concentration ;—embarrassing therefore rather than dangerous. If reminded of Varus and his lost legions, he would ask of what importance, in the story of a world-power could be the loss of a few thousand men surprised at a distance from their base amid the entanglements of a difficult and unknown country. Never, it would seem, was Empire more fortunately circumstanced for purposes of home defence.

But (it might be thought) the burden of securing frontiers of such length, even against merely tribal assaults, though easy from a strictly military point of view, might prove too heavy to be long endured. Yet the military forces scattered through the Roman Empire, though apparently adequate in the days of her greatness would, according to modern ideas, seem hardly sufficient for purposes of police, let alone defence. An army corps or less was deemed enough to preserve what are now mighty kingdoms, from internal disorder and external aggression. And if we compare with this the contributions, either in the way of money or of men, exacted from the territories subject to Rome before the Empire came into being, or at any period of the world's history since it dissolved away, the comparison must surely be entirely in favour of the Empire.

But burdens which seem light, if measured by area, may be heavy if measured by ability to pay. Yet when has ability to pay been greater in the regions bordering the Southern and Eastern Mediterranean than under the Roman Empire? Travel round it in imagination, eastward from the Atlantic coast of Morocco till returning westward you reach the head of the Adriatic Gulf, and you will have skirted a region, still of immense natural wealth, once filled with great cities, and fertile farms, better governed during the Empire than it has ever been governed since (at least till Algeria became French and Egypt British); including among its provinces what were great states before the Roman rule, and have been great states since that rule decayed, divided by

no international jealousies, oppressed by no fear
of conquest, enterprising, cultured. Remember
that to estimate its area of taxation and recruit-
ing you must add to these regions Bulgaria,
Servia, much of Austria and Bavaria, Switzer-
land, Belgium, Italy, France, Spain, and most
of Britain, and you have conditions favourable
to military strength and economic prosperity
rarely equalled in the modern world and never
in the ancient.

Our observer however might, very rightly,
feel that a far-spreading Empire like that of
Rome, including regions profoundly differing
in race, history and religion, would be liable to
other dangers than those which arise from mere
external aggression. One of the first questions,
therefore, which he would be disposed to ask,
is whether so heterogeneous a state was not
in perpetual danger of dissolution through the
disintegrating influence of national sentiments.

He would learn probably, with a strong feeling of surprise, that with the single exception of the Jews, the constituent nations, once conquered, were not merely content to belong to the Empire, but could scarcely imagine themselves doing anything else : that the Imperial system appealed, not merely to the material needs of the component populations, but also to their imagination and their loyalty ; that Gaul, Spain, and Britain, though but recently forced within the pale of civilisation, were as faithful to the Imperial ideal as the Greek of Athens or the Hellenised Orientals of Syria ; and that neither historic memories, nor local patriotism, neither disputed succession, nor public calamities, nor administrative divisions, ever really shook the sentiment in favour of Imperial Unity. There might be more than one Emperor : but there could only be one Empire. Howsoever our observer might disapprove of the Imperial

system he would therefore have to admit that
the Empire, with all its shortcomings, its absolutism and its bureaucracy, had solved more
successfully than any government, before or
since, the problem of devising a scheme which
equally satisfied the sentiments of East and
West; which respected local feelings, encouraged local government; in which the Celt,
the Iberian, the Berber, the Egyptian, the
Asiatic, the Greek, the Illyrian, the Italian
were all at home, and which, though based on
conquest, was accepted by the conquered as
the natural organisation of the civilised world.

Rome had thus unique sources of strength.
What sources of weakness would our observer
be likely to detect behind her imposing ex-
terior? The diminution of population is the
one which has (rightly I think) most impressed
historians: and it is difficult to resist the
evidence, either of the fact, or of its disastrous

consequences. I hesitate indeed to accept without qualification the accounts given us of the progressive decay of the native Italian stock from the days of the Gracchi to the disintegration of the Empire in the West; and when we read how the dearth of men was made good (in so far as it was made good) by the increasing inflow of slaves and adventurers from every corner of the known world, one wonders *whose* sons they were who, for three centuries and more, so brilliantly led the van of modern European culture, as it emerged from the darkness of the early Middle Ages. Passing by such collateral issues, however, and admitting depopulation to have been both real and serious, we may well ask whether it was not the result of Roman decadence rather than its cause, the symptom of some deep-seated social malady, not its origin. We are not concerned here with the aristocracy of Rome, nor even with the people of Italy. We are concerned with the Empire. We are not concerned with a passing phase or fashion, but with a process which seems to have gone on with increasing rapidity, through good times as well as bad, till the final cataclysm. A local disease might have a local explanation, a transient one might be due to a chance coincidence. But what can we say of a disease which was apparently co-extensive with Imperial civilisation in area, and which exceeded it in duration?

I find it hard to believe that either a selfish aversion to matrimony or a mystical admiration for celibacy, though at certain periods the one was common in Pagan and the other in Christian circles, were more than elements in the complex of causes by which the result was brought about. Like the plagues which devastated Europe in the second and third centuries, they must have greatly aggravated the evil, but they are hardly sufficient to account for it. Nor yet can we find an explanation of it in the discouragement, the sense of impending doom, by which men's spirits were oppressed long before the Imperial power began visibly to wane, for this is one of the things which, if historically true, does itself most urgently require explanation.

It may be however that our wandering politician would be too well grounded in Malthusian economics to regard a diminution of population as in itself an overwhelming calamity. And if he were pressed to describe the weak spots in the Empire of the Antonines he would be disposed, I think, to look for them on the ethical rather than on the military, the economic, or the strictly political sides of social life. He would be inclined to say, as in effect Mr Lecky does say, that in the institution of slavery, in the brutalities of the gladiatorial shows, in the gratuitous distribution of bread to the urban mobs, are to be found the corrupting influences which first weakened and then destroyed the vigour of the State.

I confess that I cannot easily accept this analysis of the facts. As regards the gladiatorial shows, even had they been universal throughout the Empire, and had they flourished more rankly as its power declined, I should still have questioned the propriety of attributing too far-reaching effects to such a cause. The Romans were brutal while they were conquering the world: its conquest enabled them to be brutal with ostentation; but we must not measure the ill consequences of their barbaric tastes by the depth of our own disgusts, nor assume the Gothic invasions to be the natural and fitting Nemesis of so much spectacular shedding of innocent blood.

As for the public distributions of corn, one would wish to have more evidence as to its social effects. But even without fully accepting the theory of the latest Roman historian, who believes that, under the then prevailing conditions of transport, no very large city could exist in Antiquity, if the supply of its food were left to private enterprise, we cannot seriously regard this practice, strange as it seems to us, as an important element in the problem. Granting for the sake of argument that it demoralised the mob of Rome, it must be remembered that Rome was not the Empire, nor did the mob of Rome govern the Empire, as once it had governed the Republic.

Slavery is a far more important matter. The magnitude of its effects on ancient societies, difficult as these are to disentangle, can hardly be exaggerated. But with what plausibility can we find in it the cause of

Rome's decline, seeing that it was the con-comitant also of its rise? How can that which in Antiquity was common to every state, have this exceptional and malign influence upon one? It would not in any case be easy to accept such a theory; but surely it becomes impossible when we bear in mind the enormous improvement effected under the Empire both in the law and the practice of slavery. Great as were its evils, they were diminishing evils—less ruinous as time went on to the character of the master, less painful and degrading to the slave. Who can believe that this immemorial custom could, in its decline, destroy a civilisation, which, in its vigour, it had helped to create?

Of course our observer would see much in the social system he was examining which he would rightly regard as morally detestable and politically pernicious. But the real question

before him would not be 'are these things good
or bad?' but 'are these things getting better
or getting worse?' And surely in most cases
he would be obliged to answer 'getting better.'
Many things moreover would come under his
notice fitted to move his admiration in a much
less qualified manner. Few governments have
been more anxious to foster an alien and higher
culture, than was the Roman Government to
foster Greek civilisation. In so far as Rome
inherited what Alexander conquered, it carried
out the ideal which Alexander had conceived.
In few periods have the rich been readier to
spend of their private fortunes on public objects.
There never was a community in which associations for every purpose of mutual aid
or enjoyment sprang more readily into existence. There never was a military monarchy
less given to wars of aggression. There never
was an age in which there was a more rapid

advance in humanitarian ideals, or a more
anxious seeking after spiritual truth. There
was much discussion, there was, apart from
politics, but little intolerance. Education was
well endowed, and its professors held in high
esteem. Physical culture was cared for. Law
was becoming scientific. Research was not
forgotten. What more could be reasonably
expected ?

According to our ordinary methods of
analysis it is not easy to say what more *could*
be reasonably expected. But plainly much more
was required. In a few generations from the
time of which I am speaking the Empire lost
its extraordinary power of assimilating alien and
barbaric elements. It became too feeble either
to absorb or to expel them : and the immigrants
who in happier times might have bestowed
renewed vigour on the commonwealth, became,
in the hour of its decline, a weakness and a

peril. Poverty grew as population shrank. Municipal office, once so eagerly desired, became the most cruel of burdens. Associations connected with industry or commerce, which began by freely exchanging public service for public privilege, found their members subjected to ever increasing obligations, for the due performance of which they and their children were liable in person and in property. Thus while Christianity, and the other forces that made for mercy, were diminishing the slavery of the slave, the needs of the Bureaucracy compelled it to trench ever more and more upon the freedom of the free. It was each man's duty (so ran the argument) to serve the commonwealth : he could best serve the commonwealth by devoting himself to his calling if it were one of public necessity : this duty he should be required under penalties to perform, and to devote if necessary to its performance, labour to the limits of endurance, fortune to the last shilling, and family to the remotest generation. Through this crude experiment in socialism, the civilised world seemed to be rapidly moving towards a system of universal caste, imposed by no immemorial custom, supported by no religious scruple, but forced on an unwilling people by the Emperor's edict and the executioner's lash.

These things have severally and collectively been regarded as the causes why in the West the Imperial system so quickly crumbled into chaos. And so no doubt they were. But they obviously require themselves to be explained by causes more general and more remote; and what were these? If I answer as I feel disposed to answer—Decadence—you will properly ask how the unknown becomes less unknown merely by receiving a name. I reply that if there be indeed subtle changes in the social tissues of old communities which make them, as time goes on, less resistant to the external attacks and the internal disturbances by which all communities are threatened, overt recognition of the fact is a step in advance. We have not an idea of what 'life' consists in, but if on that account we were to abstain from using the term, we should not be better but worse equipped for dealing with the problems of physiology; while on the other hand if we could translate life into terms of matter and motion to-morrow, we should still be obliged to use the word in order to distinguish the material movements which constitute life or exhibit it, from those which do not. In like manner we are ignorant of the inner character of the cell changes which produce senescence. But should we be better fitted to form a correct conception of the life-history of complex organisms if we refused to recognise any cause of death but accident or disease? I admit, of course, that the term 'decadence' is less precise than 'old age': as sociology deals with organisms far less definite than biology. I admit also that it explains nothing. If its use is to be justified at all, the justification must depend not on the fact that it supplies an explanation, but on the fact that it rules out explanations which are obvious but inadequate. And this may be a service of some importance. The facile generalisations with which we so often season the study of dry historic fact; the habits of political discussion which induce us to catalogue for purposes of debate the outward signs that distinguish (as we are prone to think) the standing from the falling state, hide the obscurer, but more potent, forces which silently prepare the fate of empires. National character is subtle and elusive; not to be expressed in statistics nor measured by the rough methods which suffice the practical moralist or statesman. And

when through an ancient and still powerful
state there spreads a mood of deep discouragement, when the reaction against recurring ills
grows feebler, and the ship rises less buoyantly
to each succeeding wave, when learning lan-
guishes, enterprise slackens, and vigour ebbs
away, then, as I think, there is present some
process of social degeneration, which we must
perforce recognise, and which, pending a satisfactory analysis, may conveniently be distinguished by the name of 'decadence.'

I am well aware that though the space I
have just devoted to the illustration of my
theme provided by Roman history is out of all
proportion to the general plan of this address,
yet the treatment of it is inadequate and perhaps
unconvincing. But those who are most re-
luctant to admit that decay, as distinguished
from misfortune, may lower the general level
of civilisation, can hardly deny that in many

cases that level may for indefinite periods shew no tendency to rise. If decadence be unknown, is not progress exceptional? Consider the changing politics of the unchanging East[1]. Is it not true that there, while wars and revolutions, dynastic and religious, have shattered ancient states and brought new ones into being, every community, as soon as it has risen above the tribal and nomad condition, adopts with the rarest exceptions a form of government which, from its very generality in Eastern lands, we habitually call an 'oriental despotism'? We may crystallise and re-crystallise a soluble salt as often as we please, the new crystals will always resemble the old ones. The crystals, indeed, may be of different sizes, their component

---

[1] The 'East' is a term most loosely used. It does not here include China and Japan and *does* include parts of Africa. The observations which follow have no reference either to the Jews or to the commercial aristocracies of Phœnician origin.

molecules may occupy different positions within the crystalline structure, but the structure itself will be of one immutable pattern. So it is, or seems to be, with these oriental states. They rise, in turn, upon the ruins of their predecessors, themselves predestined to perish by a like fate. But whatever their origin or history, they are always either autocracies or aggregations of autocracies; and no differences of race, of creed, or of language seem sufficient to vary the violent monotony of their internal history. In the eighteenth century theorists were content to attribute the political servitude of the Eastern world to the unscrupulous machinations of tyrants and their tools. And such explanations are good as far as they go. But this, in truth, is not very far. Intrigue, assassination, ruthless repression, the whole machinery of despotism supply particular explanations of particular incidents. They do not supply the general explanation of the general phenomenon. They tell you how this ruler or that obtained absolute power. They do not tell you why every ruler is absolute. Nor can I furnish the answer. The fact remains that over large and relatively civilised portions of the world popular government is profoundly unpopular, in the sense that it is no natural or spontaneous social growth. Political absolutism not political freedom is the familiar weed of the country. Despots change but despotism remains : and if through alien influences, like those exercised by Greek cities in Asia, or by British rule in India, the type is modified, it may well be doubted whether the modification could long survive the moment when its sustaining cause was withdrawn.

Now it would almost seem as if in lands where this political type was normal a certain level of culture (not of course the same in each case) could not permanently be overpassed. If under the excitement of religion or conquest, or else through causes more complicated and more obscure, this limit has sometimes been left behind, reaction has always followed, and decadence set in. Many people indeed, as I have already observed, take this as a matter of course. It seems to them the most natural thing in the world that the glories of the Eastern Khalifate should decay, and that the Moors in Morocco should lose even the memory of the learning and the arts possessed but three centuries ago by the Moors in Spain. To me it seems mysterious. But whether it be easy of comprehension or difficult, if only it be true, does it not furnish food for disquieting re- flexion ? If there are whole groups of nations capable on their own initiative of a certain measure of civilisation, but capable apparently of no more, and if below them again there are (as I suppose) other races who seem incapable of either creating a civilisation of their own, or of preserving unaided a civilisation impressed upon them from without, by what right do we assume that no impassable limits bar the path of Western progress? Those limits may not yet be in sight. Surely they are not. But does not a survey of history suggest that somewhere in the dim future they await our approach?

It may be replied that the history of Rome, on which I dwelt a moment ago, shews that arrested progress, and even decadence, may be but the prelude to a new period of vigorous growth. So that even those races or nations which seem frozen into eternal immobility may base upon experience their hopes of an awakening spring.

I am not sure, however, that this is the true interpretation of the facts. There is no spectacle indeed in all history more impressive than the thick darkness settling down over Western Europe, blotting out all but a faint and distorted vision of Graeco-Roman culture, and then, as it slowly rises, unveiling the variety and rich promise of the modern world. But I do not think we should make this unique phenomenon support too weighty a load of theory. I should not infer from it that when some wave of civilisation has apparently spent its force, we have a right to regard its with-drawing sweep as but the prelude to a new advance. I should rather conjecture that in this particular case we should find, among other subtle causes of decadence, some obscure dis-harmony between the Imperial system and the temperament of the West, undetected even by those who suffered from it. That system, though accepted with contentment and even with pride, though in the days of its greatness it brought civilisation, commerce, and security in its train, must surely have lacked some elements which are needed to foster among Teutons, Celts, and Iberians the qualities, whatever these may be, on which sustained progress depends. It was perhaps too oriental for the occident, and it certainly became more oriental as time went on. In the East it was, comparatively speaking, successful. If there was no progress, decadence was slow; and but for what Western Europe did, and what it failed to do, during the long struggle with militant Mahommedanism, there might still be an Empire in the East, largely Asiatic in population, Christian in religion, Greek in culture Roman by political descent.

Had this been the course of events large portions of mankind would doubtless have been much better governed than they are. It is not so clear that they would have been more 'progressive.' Progress is with the West : with communities of the European type. And if *their* energy of development is some day to be exhausted, who can believe that there remains any external source from which it can be renewed ? Where are the untried races competent to construct out of the ruined fragments of our civilisation a new and better habitation for the spirit of man ? They do not exist : and if the world is again to be buried under a barbaric flood, it will not be like that which fertilised, though it first destroyed, the western provinces of Rome, but like that which in Asia submerged for ever the last traces of Hellenic culture.

We are thus brought back to the question I put a few moments since. What grounds are there for supposing that we can escape the fate to which other races have had to submit ? If for periods which, measured on the historic scale, are of great duration, communities which have advanced to a certain point appear able to advance no further; if civilisations wear out, and races become effete, why should we expect to progress indefinitely, why for us alone is the doom of man to be reversed ?

To these questions I have no very satisfactory answers to give, nor do I believe that our knowledge of national or social psychology is sufficient to make a satisfactory answer possible. Some purely tentative observations on the point may, however, furnish a fitting conclusion to an address which has been tentative throughout, and aims rather at suggesting trains of thought, than at completing them.

I assume that the factors which combine to make each generation what it is at the moment of its entrance into adult life are in the main twofold. The one produces the raw material of society, the process of manufacture

is effected by the other. The first is physiological inheritance, the second is the inheritance
partly of external conditions of life, partly of
beliefs[1], traditions, sentiments, customs, laws,
and organisation—all that constitute the social
surroundings in which men grow up to maturity.

I hazard no conjecture as to the share borne
respectively by these two kinds of cause in pro-
ducing their joint result. Nor are we likely to
obtain satisfactory evidence on the subject till,
in the interests of science, two communities of
different blood and different traditions consent
to exchange their children at birth by a universal
process of reciprocal adoption. But even in the
absence of so heroic an experiment, it seems safe
to say that the mobility which makes possible
either progress or decadence, resides rather
in the causes grouped under the second head
than in the physiological material on which

[1] Beliefs include knowledge.

education, in the widest sense of that ambiguous term, has got to work. If, as I suppose, acquired qualities are not inherited, the only causes which could fundamentally modify the physiological character of any particular community are its intermixture with alien races through slavery, conquest, or immigration; or else new conditions which varied the relative proportion in which different sections of the population contributed to its total numbers. If, for example, the more successful members of the community had smaller families than the less successful; or if medical administration succeeded in extinguishing maladies to which persons of a particular constitution were specially liable; or if one strain in a mixed race had a larger birth rate than another— in these cases and in others like them, there would doubtless be a change in the physiological factor of national character. But such changes are not likely, I suppose, to be considerable, except, perhaps, those due to the mixture of races ;—and that only in new countries whose economic opportunities tempt immigrants widely differing in culture, and in capacity for culture, from those whose citizenship they propose to share.

The flexible element in any society, that which is susceptible of progress or decadence, must therefore be looked for rather in the physical and psychical conditions affecting the life of its component units, than in their inherited constitution. This last rather supplies a limit to variations than an element which does itself vary : though from this point of view its importance is capital. I at least find it quite impossible to believe that any attempt to provide widely different races with an identical environment, political, religious, educational, what you will, can ever make them alike.

They have been different and unequal since history began; different and unequal they are destined to remain through future periods of comparable duration.

But though the advance of each community is thus limited by its inherited aptitudes, I do not suppose that those limits have ever been reached by its unaided efforts. In the cases where a forward movement has died away, the pause must in part be due to arrested development in the variable, not to a fixed resistance in the unchanging factor of national character. Either external conditions are unfavourable; or the sentiments, customs and beliefs which make society possible have hardened into shapes which make its further self-development impossible; or through mere weariness of spirit the community resigns itself to a contented, or perhaps a discontented, stagnation; or it shatters itself in pursuit of impossible ideals, or for other and obscurer reasons, flags in its endeavours, and falls short of possible achievement.

Now I am quite unable to offer any such general analysis of the causes by which these hindrances to progress are produced or removed as would furnish a reply to my question. But it may be worth noting that a social force has come into being, new in magnitude if not in kind, which must favourably modify such hindrances as come under all but the last of the divisions in which I have roughly arranged them. This force is the modern alliance between pure science and industry. That on this we must mainly rely for the improvement of the material conditions under which societies live is in my opinion obvious, although no one would conjecture it from a historic survey of political controversy. Its direct moral effects are less obvious; indeed there are many most excellent people who would altogether deny their existence. To regard it as a force fitted to rouse and sustain the energies of nations would seem to them absurd : for this would be to rank it with those other forces which have most deeply stirred the emotions of great communities, have urged them to the greatest exertions, have released them most effectually from the benumbing fetters of merely personal preoccupations,—with religion, patriotism, and politics. Industrial expansion under scientific inspiration, so far from deserving praise like this, is in their view, at best, but a new source of material well-being, at worst the prolific parent of physical ugliness in many forms, machine made wares, smoky cities, polluted rivers, and desecrated landscapes,— appropriately associated with materialism and greed.

I believe this view to be utterly misleading, confounding accident with essence, transient accompaniments with inseparable characteristics. Should we dream of thus judging the other great social forces of which I have spoken? Are we to ignore what religion has done for the world because it has been the fruitful excuse for the narrowest bigotries and the most cruel persecutions? Are we to underrate the worth of politics, because politics may mean no more than the mindless clash of factions, or the barren exchange of one set of tyrants or jobbers for another? Is patriotism to be despised because its manifestations have been sometimes vulgar, sometimes selfish, sometimes brutal, sometimes criminal? Estimates like these seem to me worse than useless. All great social forces are not merely capable of perversion, they are constantly perverted. Yet were they eliminated from our social system, were each man, acting on the advice, which Voltaire gave but never followed, to disinterest himself of all that goes on beyond the limits of his own cabbage garden, decadence I take it, would have already far advanced.

But if the proposition I am defending may be wrongly criticised, it is still more likely to be wrongly praised. To some it will commend itself as a eulogy on an industrial as distin-guished from a military civilisation : as a suggestion that in the peaceful pursuit of wealth there is that which of itself may constitute a valuable social tonic. This may be true, but it is not my contention. In talking of the alliance between industry and science my em-phasis is at least as much on the word science as on the word industry. I am not concerned now with the proportion of the population devoted to productive labour, or the esteem in which they are held. It is on the effects which I believe are following, and are going in yet larger measure to follow, from the intimate relation between scientific discovery and industrial efficiency, that I most desire to insist.

Do you then, it will be asked, so highly rate the utilitarian aspect of research as to regard it as a source, not merely of material convenience, but of spiritual elevation ? Is it seriously to be ranked with religion and patriotism as an important force for raising men's lives above what is small, personal, and self-centred ? Does it not rather pervert pure knowledge into a new contrivance for making money, and give a fresh triumph to the 'growing materialism of the age' ?

I do not myself believe that this age is either less spiritual or more sordid than its predecessors. I believe, indeed, precisely the reverse. But however this may be, is it not plain that if a society is to be moved by the remote speculations of isolated thinkers it can only be on condition that their isolation is not complete ? Some point of contact they must have with the world in which they live, and if their influence is to be based on widespread sympathy, the contact must be in a region where there can be, if not full mutual comprehension, at least a large measure of practical agreement and willing co-operation. Philosophy has never touched the mass of men except through religion. And, though the parallel is not complete, it is safe to say that science will never touch them unaided by its practical applications. Its wonders may be catalogued for purposes of education, they may be illustrated by arresting experiments, by numbers and magnitudes which startle or fatigue the imagination ; but they will form no familiar portion of the intellectual furniture of ordinary men unless they be connected, however remotely, with the conduct of ordinary life. Critics have made merry over the naive self-importance which represented man as the centre and final cause of the universe, and conceived the stupendous mechanism of nature as primarily designed to satisfy his wants and minister to his entertainment. But there is another, and an opposite, danger into which it is possible to fall. The material world, howsoever it may have gained in sublimity, has, under the touch of science, lost (so to speak) in domestic charm. Except where it affects the immediate needs of organic life, it may seem so remote from the concerns of men that in the majority it will rouse no curiosity, while of those who are fascinated by its marvels, not a few will be chilled by its impersonal and indifferent immensity.

For this latter mood only religion or religious philosophy can supply a cure. But for the former, the appropriate remedy is the perpetual stimulus which the influence of science on the business of mankind offers to their sluggish curiosity. And even now I believe this influence to be underrated. If in the last hundred years the whole material setting of civilised life has altered, we owe it neither to politicians nor to political institutions. We owe it to the combined efforts of those who have advanced science and those who have applied it. If our outlook upon the Universe has suffered modifications in detail so great and so numerous that they amount collectively to a revolution, it is to men of science we owe it, not to theologians or philosophers. On these indeed new and weighty responsibilities are being cast. They have to harmonise and to coordinate, to prevent the new from being one-sided, to preserve the valuable essence of what is old. But science is the great instrument of social change, all the greater because its object is not change but knowledge;

and its silent appropriation of this dominant function, amid the din of political and religious strife, is the most vital of all the revolutions which have marked the development of modern civilisation.

It may seem fanciful to find in a single recent aspect of this revolution an influence which resembles religion or patriotism in its appeals to the higher side of ordinary characters—especially since we are accustomed to regard the appropriation by industry of scientific discoveries merely as a means of multiplying the material conveniences of life. But if it be remembered that this process brings vast sections of every industrial community into admiring relation with the highest intellectual achievement, and the most disinterested search for truth; that those who live by ministering to the common wants of average humanity lean for support on those who search among the deepest mysteries of Nature ; that their dependence is rewarded by growing success ; that success gives in its turn an incentive to individual effort in no wise to be measured by personal expectation of gain ; that the energies thus aroused may affect the whole character of the community, spreading the beneficent contagion of hope and high endeavour through channels scarcely known, to workers[1] in fields the most remote; if all this be borne in mind it may perhaps seem not unworthy of the place I have assigned to it.

But I do not offer this speculation, whatever be its worth, as an answer to my original question. It is but an aid to optimism, not a reply to pessimism. Such a reply can only be given by a sociology which has arrived at scientific conclusions on the life-history of different types of society, and has risen above

---

[1] See note at the end of the paper.

the empirical and merely interrogative point of
view which, for want of a better, I have adopted
in this address. No such sociology exists at
present, or seems likely soon to be created.
In its absence the conclusions at which I
provisionally arrive are that we cannot regard
decadence and arrested development as less
normal in human communities than progress;
though the point at which the energy of advance
is exhausted (if, and when it is reached) varies
in different races and civilisations: that the
internal causes by which progress is encouraged,
hindered, or reversed, lie to a great extent
beyond the field of ordinary political discussion, and are not easily expressed in current
political terminology: that the influence which a
superior civilisation, whether acting by example
or imposed by force, may have in advancing
an inferior one, though often beneficent, is not
likely to be self supporting; its withdrawal will

be followed by decadence, unless the character
of the civilisation be in harmony both with the
acquired temperament and the innate capacities
of those who have been induced to accept it :
that as regards those nations which still advance
in virtue of their own inherent energies, though
time has brought perhaps new causes of disquiet,
it has brought also new grounds of hope ; and
that whatever be the perils in front of us, there
are, so far, no symptoms either of pause or of
regression in the onward movement which for
more than a thousand years has been character-
istic of Western civilisation.

NOTE TO PAGE 57.

This remark arises out of a train of thought suggested
by two questions which are very pertinent to the subject
of the Address.

(1) Is a due succession of men above the average
in original capacity necessary to maintain social progress ?
and

(2) If so, can we discover any law according to which
such men are produced ?

I entertain no doubt myself that the answer to the first question should be in the affirmative. Democracy is an excellent thing; but, though quite consistent with progress, it is not progressive *per se*. Its value is regulative not dynamic; and if it meant (as it never does) substantial uniformity, instead of legal equality, we should become fossilised at once. Movement may be controlled or checked by the many; it is initiated and made effective by the few. If (for the sake of illustration) we suppose mental capacity in all its many forms to be mensurable and commensurable, and then imagine two societies possessing the same average capacity—but an average made up in one case of equal units, in the other of a majority slightly below the average and a minority much above it, few could doubt that the second, not the first, would show the greatest aptitude for movement. It might go wrong, but it would go.

The second question—how is this originality (in its higher manifestations called genius) effectively produced? is not so simple.

Excluding education in its narrowest sense—which few would regard as having much to do with the matter—the only alternatives seem to be the following:

Original capacity may be no more than one of the ordinary variations incidental to heredity. A community may breed a minority thus exceptionally gifted, as it breeds a minority of men over six feet six. There may be an average decennial output of congenital geniuses as there is an average decennial output of congenital idiots—though the number is likely to be smaller.

But if this be the sole cause of the phenomenon, why does the same race *apparently* produce many men of genius in one generation and few in another? Why are years of abundance so often followed by long periods of sterility?

The most obvious explanation of this would seem to be that in some periods circumstances give many openings to genius, in some periods few. The genius is constantly produced ; but it is only occasionally recognised.

In this there must be some truth. A mob orator in Turkey, a religious reformer in seventeenth century Spain, a military leader in the Sandwich islands, would hardly get their chance. Yet the theory of opportunity can scarcely be reckoned a complete explanation. For it leaves un-accounted for the *variety* of genius which has in some countries marked epochs of vigorous national development. Athens in the fifth and fourth centuries, Florence in the fifteenth and early sixteenth centuries, Holland in the later sixteenth and seventeenth centuries, are the typical examples. In such periods the opportunities of statesmen, soldiers, orators, and diplomatists, may have been specially frequent. But whence came the poets, the sculptors, the painters, the philosophers and the men of letters? What peculiar opportunities had *they*?

The only explanation, if we reject the idea of a mere coincidence, seems to be, that quite apart from opportunity, the exceptional stir and fervour of national life evokes or may evoke qualities which in ordinary times lie dormant, unknown even to their possessors. The potential Miltons are 'mute' and 'inglorious' not because they cannot find a publisher, but because they have nothing they want to publish. They lack the kind of inspiration which, on this view, flows from social surroundings where great things, though of quite another kind, are being done and thought.

If this theory be true (and it is not without its difficulties) one would like to know whether these un-doubted outbursts of originality in the higher and rarer form of genius, are symptomatic of a general rise in the number of persons exhibiting original capacity of a more ordinary type. If so, then the conclusion would seem to be that some kind of widespread exhilaration or excitement is required in order to enable any community to extract the best results from the raw material transmitted to it by natural inheritance.

Printed in the United States
By Bookmasters